# The Littl
# of Traditic

## by Marianne Sargent
## Illustrations by Marion Lindsay

**LITTLE BOOKS WITH BIG IDEAS**

Reprinted 2011
Published 2010 by A&C Black Publishers Limited
36 Soho Square, London W1D 3QY
www.acblack.com

ISBN 978-1-4081-2328-7


Text © Marianne Sargent, 2010
Illustrations © Marion Lindsay, 2010
Cover photographs © Shutterstock

Printed in Great Britain by Latimer Trend & Company Limited

This book is produced using paper that is made from wood grown in
managed, sustainable forests. It is natural, renewable and recyclable.

The logging and manufacturing processes conform to the environmental
regulations of the country of origin.

**To see our full range of titles
visit www.acblack.com**

# Contents

# Introduction

This book is aimed at early years practitioners working with young children in Foundation Stage settings as well as teachers working in Key Stage 1. It is intended as a resource to support the thematic use of traditional tales.

## The magic of traditional tales

Traditional tales transport children into a world of infinite possibility. Talking animals, personified objects and magical happenings encourage them to suspend their disbelief and become carried away by the thrill of fantastical events. Such stories foster imaginative thought and creativity within children. The familiar nature of the tales and wide availability of supporting resources, including puppets and masks, makes them ideal for creative exploration, such as retelling them and acting them out.

"Children's creativity must be extended by the provision of support for their curiosity, exploration and play. They must be provided with opportunities to explore and share their thoughts, ideas and feelings..." (DCSF, 2008, Practice Guidance for the Foundation Stage, CD card).

The genre is particularly useful for teaching about story structure, character and setting. There are many different versions of these stories in existence and children can formulate their own plots, add new characters and offer suggestions for alternative endings. Being encouraged to play with and experiment with stories is excellent preparation for later reading and writing.

Throughout this book there are suggestions for activities that aim to promote an enjoyment of stories within young children, offering age-appropriate experiences that aim to lay the foundations of literacy.

## The oral tradition

'Storytelling is a powerful way to develop children's speaking and listening skills, and anybody can do it! You don't have to be an extrovert, you don't need any special qualifications and it doesn't matter if you make a mistake – the children will revel in your blunders and enjoy putting you right!' (Ros Bayley and Sue Palmer, 2004, Foundations of Literacy).

Historically, traditional tales were passed on orally from one generation to the next and it follows that they are still a fantastic genre for telling without a text. Storytelling in this way requires children to use their imaginations. Most children are already familiar with these stories and this, along with the storyteller's actions and gestures, enables them to build a picture in their own minds. Furthermore, the repetitive style, which can be exaggerated in the telling, inspires children to join in, thus encouraging attentive listening.

Most of the tales featured are available as audio versions. In addition, throughout the book there are suggestions for poems, songs and rhymes that can be associated with each story. Singing and acting out rhymes not only enhances the enjoyment of stories, but also promotes speech and language development.

## Personal, Social and Emotional Development

According to the requirements set out by the Practice Guidance for the Early Years Foundation Stage, 'children must be provided with experiences and support which will help them to develop a positive sense of themselves and of others' (DCSF, 2008, PSED card). Traditional tales have central themes relating to moral messages that can be explored and discussed, aiding personal, social and emotional development.

Traditional tales explore some of the most important issues in life! Questions about the relationship between good and evil, the value of loyalty and the importance of helping each other are all themes that are explored in these stories. Discussing these narratives with children helps them to think deeply about such things, offering their opinions, sharing ideas and developing understandings about motivation, character and plot.' (Helen Bromley, Early Years Consultant.)

For each story featured in this book a moral is suggested and a PSED Focus that is directly related to the EYFS is provided along with the other links with the EYFS areas of learning and development.

## Using the book

This book features thirty traditional tales. For each you will find:

▶ The tale's origin and 'moral of the story'

▶ Suggested activities related to the tale

▶ The relevant learning intentions covered in undertaking these activities, including a PSED focus

▶ A list of songs, rhymes and poems

▶ An investigation area section

▶ Alternate versions to the original tale.

## Useful generic activities

Here are some ideas for enhancing any of the traditional tales featured in this book:

▶ Read through each story carefully. Consider the actions of the various characters and think of some open questions about the different moral dilemmas that arise.

▶ Set up role-play and small world scenes related to the stories.

▶ Encourage children to empathise or identify with different characters by asking them how they would feel if in their position.

▶ Play hot-seating games – take on the persona of a character and encourage the children to ask you questions.

▶ Reverse roles – ask children to become the characters and ask them questions.

▶ Dress up as the characters and act out the story.

▶ Put on a puppet show.

▶ Make character posters; draw/paint pictures and include a simple description – think of adjectives to describe personality.

▶ Make up rhymes about the characters.

▶ Draw a story map detailing the order of events in the plot.

▶ Make a 3D frieze of the story using junk material and mod-roc.

▶ Make a large scale board game featuring the story plot and characters.

▶ Make an electronic book using PowerPoint, Smart Notebook or other presentation software.

▶ Read alternative versions of the stories and ask the children which they prefer and why.

▶ Choose musical instruments and make different sounds to represent the personalities of characters.

▶ Consider what might happen if the characters from two different stories met each other.

## Useful generic resources

For each of the stories in this book it would be useful to collect:

▶ character face masks and costumes for role-play and drama

▶ finger puppets or character figures for small world play

▶ hand puppets and pop up theatre to act out the story.

# General areas of learning and development covered through the use of traditional tales

Although the specific learning intentions linked to the suggested activities are provided, the Little Book of Traditional Tales covers the following early learning goals:

## Personal, social and emotional development (PSED):

▶ Continue to be interested, excited and motivated to learn.

▶ Maintain attention, concentrate and sit quietly when appropriate.

▶ Understand what is right, what is wrong and why.

▶ Consider the consequences of their words and actions for themselves and others.

▶ Understand that people have different views, cultures and beliefs, that need to be treated with respect.

▶ Select and use activities and resources independently.

## Communication, language and literacy (CLL):

▶ Listen with enjoyment and respond to stories, songs and other music, rhymes and poems and make up their own stories, rhymes and poems.

▶ Use language to imagine and recreate roles and experiences.

▶ Explore and experiment with sounds, words and texts.

▶ Retell narratives in the correct sequence, drawing on the language patterns of stories.

▶ Show an understanding of the elements of stories, such as main character, sequence of events and openings and how information can be found in non-fiction texts to answer questions about where, who, why and how.

## Knowledge and understanding of the world (KUW):

▶ Begin to know about their own cultures and beliefs and those of other people.

## Creative development (CD):

▶ Sing simple songs from memory, recognise repeated sounds and sound patterns and match movements to music.

▶ Use their imagination in music, imaginative and role-play and stories.

▶ Express and communicate their ideas, thoughts and feelings by using imaginative and role-play and songs.

# Little Red Riding Hood

Origin – The Brothers Grimm    Moral – Beware of strangers

## Activities to follow up the story

▶ Use the story as a starting point for discussion about talking to strangers.

▶ Use a red hooded cloak for a listening game; a child conceals themselves, and others listen to the voice and guess their identity.

▶ Use a basket and some picnic items to play a memory game; "I went to Grandma's house and in my basket I took..."

▶ Weave baskets.

▶ Make real sandwiches with healthy fillings for Grandma's basket; do a survey to find out the most popular sandwich and create a pictogram using a computer program such as 2Count (2Simple Software) to present the results.

▶ Visit some woods – find out about the local wildlife.

▶ Play "What's the time Mr Wolf?" and show the time on a real clock face.

▶ Have a picnic role-play outdoors or Grandma's house role-play indoors.

▶ Have a small world wood with toy trees, woodchip and wolves.

▶ Sponge print wolves' paw prints with black, white, grey and brown paints.

## Songs, rhymes and poems

Little Red Riding Hood and the Wolf by Roald Dahl (Revolting Rhymes, Puffin books)

Winter Trees by Zoltan Zelk (The New Faber Book of Children's Poems)

## Investigation area

If you go down to the woods:
1. Collect natural woodland items, e.g. leaves, twigs, pine cones, maple tree seeds (helicopters), stones.
2. Supply close observation equipment such as magnifiers and set up a digital microscope.
3. Provide some sorting hoops for sorting leaves according to colour and shape.
4. Display non-fiction books about woodland wildlife.

### Alternate versions to the original tale

Little Red Riding Hood by Sam McBratney & Emma Chichester Clark – in this version Grandma is locked in a cupboard and Red Riding Hood is eaten. They are rescued by the woodcutter.

Little Red Riding Hood by Josephine Evetts-Secker & Nicoletta Ceccoli – in this version both Grandma and Red Riding Hood are eaten before being rescued by a huntsman.

Pretty Salma by Niki Daly – set in West India with a big bad dog instead of a wolf.

## Links with the EYFS Areas of Learning and Development

PSED: Begin to recognise danger and know who to turn to for help; show a strong sense of self as a member of their family.

CLL: Sustain attentive listening; speak clearly and audibly with confidence and control.

PSRN: Count reliably up to ten everyday objects; begin to make comparisons between quantities; use everyday language related to time.

KUW: Investigate objects and materials by using all of their senses as appropriate; complete a simple program on a computer.

PD: Engage in activities that require hand-eye coordination; manipulate materials to achieve a planned effect.

CD: Engage in imaginative play and role-play; create printed paintings.

# The Hare and the Tortoise

Origin – Aesop's fable    Moral – Slow and steady wins the race

## Activities to follow up the story

▶ Circle time – ask the children to think about what they are good at and what they are not so good at. Talk about how different people are good at different things.

▶ Find out about hares – what is the difference between a rabbit and a hare?

▶ Race like the hare and the tortoise – use a selection of timers to time the children racing like different animals, e.g. hop like a hare, crawl like a tortoise. Compare the timings.

▶ Use the Internet to find examples of different animals that move at varying speeds in contrasting ways, e.g. flying, swimming, slithering, crawling, running, swinging.

▶ Set up an outdoor tricky races area, e.g. balancing beanbags on heads, carrying golf balls on spoons.

▶ Print tortoise shell patterns on shell shaped templates with cotton reels and brown, black and green paints.

## Songs, rhymes and poems

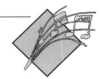

Tortoise and Hare Poem by Judith Nicholls (Midnight Forest, Faber & Faber)

A Tortoise Called Joe by Michael Palin (The Hutchinson Treasury of Children's Poetry)

The Tortoise and the Hare by Roald Dahl (Rhyme Stew, Puffin)

## Investigation area

Wacky races:

1. Set up a small race track with miniature toy animals.
2. Supply small flags, timers and stop watches for experimenting with timing.
3. Provide charts for recording race results.
4. Set out numbered sorting tubs for arranging the animals according to finishing place.

## Alternate versions to the original tale

The Race by Caroline Repchuk & Alison Jay – the hare and the tortoise race around the world using all kinds of different transportation.

Hare and Tortoise Race to the Moon by Oliver Corwin – the animals race to the moon. Hare has bought his spacecraft and tortoise had made his own.

Clever Tortoise by Francesca Martin – African traditional tale about a brainy tortoise that stands up against some bigger, stronger animals.

The Foolish Tortoise by Eric Carle – a tortoise dumps his shell in the hope that it will help him move quicker.

Jellybabys website – for a modern version of the story in audio go to www.jellybabys.co.uk/hare-tortoise.php

## Links with the EYFS Areas of Learning and Development

PSED: Begin to develop self-confidence and a belief in themselves; persist for extended periods of time at an activity.

CLL: Extend their vocabulary, exploring the meanings and sounds of new words; explore and experiment with texts.

KUW: Show curiosity and interest in the features of living things; use information and communication technology to support their learning.

PD: Move freely with pleasure and confidence in a range of ways; negotiate space successfully when playing racing games with other children.

CD: Create printed paintings.

# The Three Little Pigs

Origin - 19th century English tale   Moral – Hard work reaps reward

## Activities to follow up the story

▶ Circle time – Consider which of the three pigs' houses stayed standing and why. Think about which would have been quicker to build. What does this tell us about the worth of some more difficult tasks?

▶ Use the story as a basis for addition and subtraction activities – moving pigs in and out of houses.

▶ Role-play activity – dress up as the big bad wolf and protest your innocence. Get children to question you about what happened to the little pigs.

▶ Provide a range of items and materials for children to build a den outside.

▶ Visit a local farm.

## Songs, rhymes and poems

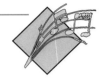

The Pig by Roald Dahl (Dirty Beasts, Puffin Books)

The House that Jack Built by Diana Mayo – picture book and CD featuring the traditional rhyme (Barefoot Books)

Find a range of poems, limericks and rhymes about pigs at www.potbellypigpets.com/poems.html

## Investigation area

Building houses:

1.  Make three small collapsible houses using painted card for the children to use as props with finger puppets or small toy characters
2.  Set out some real straw, twigs and bricks, as well as some alternative building materials, such as slate, concrete and cement for children to examine.

### Alternate versions to the original tale

The True Story of the Three Little Pigs by Jon Scieszka & Lane Smith – The story from the innocent wolf's point of view.

The Three Little Wolves and the Big Bad Pig by Eugene Trivizas & Helen Oxenbury – based on the original but with a reversal of roles.

Pigs Might Fly by Jonathan Emmet & Steve Cox – the pigs and wolf build flying machines and take part in a race.

Scary Creatures: Wolves by Penny Clarke & Bob Hersey – detailed and clear information book.

Pigs by Rachael Bell – information book explaining the life cycle of the pig with details about why pigs are reared.

## Links with the EYFS Areas of Learning and Development

PSED: Have a positive approach to activities; have an awareness of, and an interest in, cultural and religious differences.

CLL: Consistently develop a line of questioning; sustain attentive listening, responding to what they have heard with relevant comments and questions.

PSRN: In practical activities and discussion begin to use the vocabulary involved in adding and subtracting.

KUW: Investigate different foods by using all of their senses as appropriate; ask questions about why things happen and how things work; construct with a purpose in mind, using a variety of materials.

CD: Create paintings; choose colours for a particular purpose.

# Lazy Lion

Origin – Kenya    Moral – Hard work reaps reward

## Activities to follow up the story

▶ Circle time – discuss the benefits of trying hard and doing our best. Talk about the different kinds of homes the children live in; ask children to draw pictures of their homes.

▶ Challenge the children to make a waterproof home – use junk materials to make model houses and experiment with different materials (e.g. tinfoil, plastic, paper, cardboard) to create waterproof roofs.

▶ Make lion face masks with paper plates and feathers for the mane.

▶ Small world African plain in the sand tray accompanied by information books about African wildlife.

▶ Experiment with 'rain making' utensils in the water tray (sieve, watering can, flour shaker, salt and pepper pots, punctured bottles).

▶ Make rainmakers using cardboard tubes with the ends covered and filled with rice.

## Songs, rhymes and poems

The Lion by Roald Dahl (Dirty Beasts, Puffin Books)

I Hear Thunder (Early Years Poems and Rhymes, Scholastic)

Animals' Houses by James Reeves (The Oxford Treasury of Children's Poems)

## Investigation area

Outdoor animal habitat:

1. Use a hollowed log, damp leaves and soil to encourage minibeasts to move in.
2. Provide minibeast catchers and magnifiers for close inspection and clipboards and paper for note taking and drawing.
3. Display laminated (weatherproof) pictures of animal habitats.

---

### Alternate versions to the original tale

Hot Hippo, Greedy Zebra, Hungry Hyena, Tricky Tortoise, Crafty Chameleon & Baby Baboon by Mwenye Hadithi & Adrienne Kennaway – all based on traditional African stories and address a range of moral issues.

Animal Groups: Life in a Pride – Lions by Louise Spilsbury & Richard Spilsbury – information book about the family life of lions.

Roar by Margaret Mayo & Alex Ayliffe – colourful picture book featuring lions amongst a range of other African animals.

South African Animals by Lindiwe Mabuza & Alan Baker – picture book of animals and their habitats.

---

## Links with the EYFS Areas of Learning and Development

**PSED:** Have a positive approach to activities and events.

**KUW:** Observe, find out about and identify feature in the place they live and the natural environment; investigate various construction materials; construct with a purpose in mind, using a variety of resources; investigate objects and materials by using all of their senses as appropriate.

**PD:** Handle tools, and construction materials safely and with increasing control.

**CD:** Create masks using collage and paint; engage in imaginative play and role-play.

# The Gingerbread Man

Origin – American version of the European 'fleeing pancake'!
Moral – It doesn't pay to show off

## Activities to follow up the story

▶ Circle time – talk about the gingerbread man's over confidence and boastful behaviour. Consider why he ended up being eaten by the fox.

▶ Make gingerbread biscuits in the shape of people, houses, trees. Find a recipe for Gingerbread trees at www.bbcgoodfood.com/recipes/3000/gingerbread-trees. Or make some gingerbread coloured playdough and provide a variety of different shaped cutters.

▶ Experiment with dropping gingerbread in water and observe what happens; consider whether it matters if the water is hot or cold.

▶ Make gingerbread people hand puppets; use felt, add buttons for eyes and draw on further details with fabric pens.

## Songs, rhymes and poems

Gingerbread Man poem at www.dltk-teach.com

Gingerbread Man Rhymes at www.storybus.org/stories_and_activities

## Investigation area

You can't catch me, I'm the gingerbread man:
1. Draw out a map depicting the story of the gingerbread man's journey.
2. Provide small world story characters for the children to follow the map and act out the story.
3. Display different storybooks telling different versions of the story.

### Alternate versions to the original tale

The Gingerbread Boy by Paul Galdone – the story retold with humorous illustrations.

The Gingerbread Girl by Lisa Campbell Ernst – this time the old man and woman make a girl and she runs away just like her brother.

Gingerbread Baby and Gingerbread Friends by Jan Brett – the first is a similar tale to the original but features a baby. The second is a sequel.

Maisy Makes Gingerbread by Lucy Cousins – Maisy Mouse makes gingerbread for tea.

Gingerbread Land by Katie Grim, Jake Johnson & Dennis DiLaura – a book of photographs of three-dimensional scenes featuring a magical gingerbread land.

## Links with the EYFS Areas of Learning and Development

PSED: Have an awareness and pride in self as having own identity and abilities; value and contribute to own self-control; consider the consequences of their words and actions for themselves.

CLL: Begin to be aware of how stories are structured; explore and experiment with texts.

KUW: Investigate food using all of their senses as appropriate; describe and talk about what they see; show curiosity about why things happen; show understanding of cause/effect relations.

PD: Explore malleable materials; engage in activities requiring hand-eye coordination; demonstrate increasing skill and control over mark-making implements.

CD: Create puppets; understand that different media can be combined.

# Thumbelina

Origin – Hans Christian Anderson    Moral – Never give up

## Activities to follow up the story

▶ Discuss the story – talk about the trials and tribulations that Thumbelina encounters; ask the children what might have happened to her if she had just given up hope; talk about why we should always try our best even when things are difficult.

▶ Find out about small mythical creatures, such as pixies, elves and fairies; find out who believes and who doesn't and why.

▶ Hide fairies, pixies and elves all around the setting and provide simple maps or read out directional clues for the children to seek them out.

▶ Imagine what it would be like to shrink down to a tiny size; write stories or paint/draw pictures about possible adventures.

▶ Find out about the children's experience of the tooth fairy.

▶ Use junk materials to make miniature vehicles for small mythical creatures like pixies, elves and fairies.

▶ Create some number problems using toy fairies and flower cut-outs.

## Songs, rhymes and poems

Tommy Thumb, Tommy Thumb – a traditional action rhyme
(This Little Puffin, Puffin Books)

Fairy Story by Stevie Smith (The New Faber Book of Children's Poems)

Little Fairy by Brittany Graviet (www.poemhunter.com/poems/fairy/page-1/)

## Investigation area

Keep on trying:

1. Set out some activities that require perseverance, e.g. tricky jigsaw puzzles, laminated mazes with wipe-away pens, bead frames.
2. Put some sand timers out for children to make the tasks more difficult if they want to raise the challenge.
3. Provide some paper for children to sign their names when they have completed a challenge.

### Alternate versions to the original tale

Thumbelina by Brian Alderson & Hans Christian Andersen – the classic story with beautiful illustrations.

Tom and Small by Clara Vulliamy – a little boy shrinks down to a tiny size and goes on an adventure with his toy mouse.

Where the Fairies Fly by Jane Simmons – magical picture book.

Fairies by Alison Maloney & Patricia Moffett – all about the magical creatures.

Titch by Pat Hutchins – classic story about what it is like to be small.

Dear Tooth Fairy by Alan Durant & Vanessa Cabban – picture book with lots of added extras.

## Links with the EYFS Areas of Learning and Development

PSED: Begin to develop self-confidence and a belief in themselves; have a positive approach to activities and events; persist for extended periods of time at an activity of their choosing.

CLL: Speak clearly and audibly with confidence and control and show awareness of the listener; attempt writing for different purposes using features of different forms, such as stories.

KUW: Construct with a purpose in mind using a variety of resources.

PSRN: Use developing mathematical ideas and methods to solve practical problems; use everyday words to describe position.

CD: Begin to make-believe by pretending; engage in imaginative play.

# Jack and the Beanstalk

Origin – Germany   Moral – Beware of strangers

## Activities to follow up the story

▶ Discuss the story – Jack accepts some magic beans from a stranger. Consider the possible consequences of accepting things from strangers.

▶ Compare the appearance and taste of different beans; make a bean salad using different tinned beans (haricot, kidney, butter); make a bean stir-fry using different green beans (runner, broad, french).

▶ Take digital photos of the stages involved in making the above dishes and make some bean recipe cards.

▶ Plant beans and place them in different environments (dark corner, cold place, sunny spot, warm place with no daylight); observe and record what happens.

▶ Measure the length of different green beans and arrange in size order.

▶ Role-play a bean market; set out a variety of beans and price them per kilo; provide weighing scales, money, till, paper bags and note paper for receipts.

▶ Make magic beans using salt-dough or clay; paint with shiny paints and dip in glitter.

▶ Role-play a giant's castle with oversized objects and resources.

## Songs, rhymes and poems

The Sleepy Giant by Charles Edward Carryl (The Oxford Treasury of Children's Poetry)

Giant's Breakfast by Judith Nicholls – a counting rhyme (Early Years Poems and Rhymes, Scholastic)

Beans, Beans, Beans at www.101kidz.com/poems/food.html

## Investigation area

As tall as giants:

1. Involve the children in making a giant beanstalk using sugar paper and card; stick it to the wall and draw a metric measuring scale on it.
2. Provide a tub of large leaf cut-outs, pencils and blu-tack for children to measure each other against the scale, record their names on the leaves and stick onto the beanstalk.
3. Display a table of results recording names and heights and showing who is the tallest down to the shortest.

### Alternate versions to the original tale

Jim and the Beanstalk by Raymond Briggs.

Jasper's Beanstalk by Nick Butterworth & Mick Inkpen – little Jasper the cat plants a bean and waits for it to grow.

Anansi and the Pot of Beans by Bobby Norfolk, Sherry Norfolk & Baird Hoffmire – Anansi's grandma cooks a pot of spicy beans.

The Life Cycle of a Bean by Linda Tagliaferro & Gail Saunders-Smith – information book for young children.

## Links with the EYFS Areas of Learning and Development

**PSED:** Begin to recognise danger and know who to turn to for help.

**CLL:** Attempt writing for different purposes, using features of different forms such as recipe instructions and ingredients lists; use their phonic knowledge to write simple regular words and make phonetically plausible attempts at more complex words.

**PSRN:** Order two or three items by length; begin to make comparisons between quantities.

**KUW:** Investigate objects using all of their senses as appropriate; look closely at similarities and differences; know how to operate a digital camera; show understanding of cause/effect relations; ask questions about why things happen and how things work.

# The Enormous Turnip

Origin – Russian   Moral – Many hands make light work

## Activities to follow up the story

▶ Discuss the story – ask the children to consider how the mouse is initially perceived and how helpful she turns out to be.

▶ Work collaboratively to create a large wall display of all the story characters working together to pull up the turnip; ask more able children to write captions.

▶ Grow some turnips; use them to make turnip soup or stew.

▶ Find out about root vegetables; examine and taste a selection.

▶ Arrange some real root vegetables according to size.

▶ Use farm animal sorting sets to arrange different animals by size and sort into size groups.

▶ Make vegetable character pictures; cut out good quality pictures of root vegetables and stick them on paper, e.g. carrots for arms, potatoes or turnips for heads, parsnips for legs, beetroots for bodies. Stick on wiggly eyes, buttons etc  for detail.

▶ Cut patterns out of root vegetables and dip them in ready mixed paint for printing.

## Songs, rhymes and poems

The Turnip by anon (Early Years Poems and Rhymes, Scholastic)

Old MacDonald Had a Shop (This Little Puffin, Puffin Books)

The Farmer's In His Den at www.landofnurseryrhymes.co.uk

## Investigation area
The root of the problem:

1. Set out some root vegetables (carrots, potatoes, turnips, parsnips radishes, celeriac, beetroots).
2. Put the seed equivalents in bowls and challenge the children to match the vegetable to the seed.
3. Display seed packets, posters that show root vegetables growing above and below ground and information books about farming and growing crops.

---

### Alternate versions to the original tale

The Gigantic Turnip by Niamh Sharkey & Aleksei Tolstoy – a beautifully illustrated version.

Mr Wolf and the Enormous Turnip by Jan Fearnley – Mr Wolf finds an enormous turnip and thinks it would be great for making a spicy stew.

The Rather Small Turnip by Laurence Anholt & Arthur Robins – from the Seriously Silly Stories series.

From the Garden by Michael Dahl & Todd Ouren – a counting book.

Growing Vegetable Soup by Lois Ehlert – a simple picture book about growing vegetables with a recipe for vegetable soup.

Kiddie Gardens Website – for practical information about gardening with children go to www.kiddiegardens.com

---

## Links with the EYFS Areas of Learning and Development

**PSED:** Work as part of a group or class; learn social skills and enjoy being with and talking to adults and other children.

**CLL:** Write labels and captions.

**PSRN:** Begin to categorise objects according to size; order items by size.

**KUW:** Investigate objects using all of their senses as appropriate; look closely at similarities and differences; show curiosity and interest in the features of objects and living things; show curiosity about why things happen and how things work.

**PD:** Develop their own likes and dislikes in food.

**CD:** Create collages, paintings and drawings; work on a large or small scale.

# The Town Mouse and the Country Mouse

Origin – Aesop's Fable   Moral – It is all right to be different, like different things and live in a different way

## Activities to follow up the story

▶ Discuss the story – we all live different lives in different types of home with different families. Consider the idea that what suits some people, might not suit others.

▶ Circle time – talk about what scared the town and country mice; consider why they were scared, i.e. being in an unfamiliar environment; ask the children what frightens them.

▶ Take a trip to the countryside/town; take time to absorb sights, sounds and smells.

▶ Create a picture dictionary about the countryside/town; use a computer to do this, e.g. Smart Notebook software or PowerPoint.

▶ Challenge the children to design and build a small world town using Lego or Brio.

▶ Make mice finger puppet sets for counting rhymes; add eyes, noses, whiskers and bow ties to the fingertips of gloves to create five mice.

▶ Play cat and mouse chasing games.

## Songs, rhymes and poems

Three Blind Mice – traditional rhyme (Michael Foreman's Nursery Rhymes, Walker Books)

Five Little Mice Came Out to Play – counting rhyme (This Little Puffin, Puffin Books)

Three Little Mice Walked into Town by Charlotte Druitt Cole (Poems for the Very Young by Michael Rosen & Bob Graham)

## Investigation area

Town and country:

1. Supply laminated pictures from the town and countryside backed with Velcro.
2. Set up a felt board divided into two, labelled 'town' and 'country' for children to sort the pictures.
3. Display non-fiction books with information about town and countryside environments.

### Alternate versions to the original tale

Town Mouse, Country Mouse by Jan Brett – a twist on the original tale.

Tilly and Milly: The Story of the Town Mouse and the Country Mouse by Kate Summers & Maggie Kneen – the traditional tale featuring female mice.

The Tale of Johnny Town-Mouse by Beatrix Potter – A variation based on the original fable.

School Express website – for an animated version of the story go to www.schoolexpress.com/storytime/town.html

## Links with the EYFS Areas of Learning and Development

PSED: Understand that people have different needs, views, cultures and beliefs, that need to be treated with respect; have a developing awareness of their own feelings and be sensitive to the feelings of others.

CLL: Hear and say the initial sound in words and know which letters represent some of the sounds.

KUW: Look closely at similarities and differences; describe and talk about what they see; use ICT to support their learning.

PD: Demonstrate increasing skill and control in the use of construction sets and small-world activities; negotiate space successfully when playing chasing games with other children, adjusting speed or changing direction to avoid obstacles.

CD: Create finger puppets; begin to construct, stacking blocks vertically and horizontally, making enclosures and creating spaces.

# The Ugly Duckling

Origin – Hans Christian Anderson
Moral – Be proud of who you are

## Activities to follow up the story

▶ Discuss the story – talk about why it is unkind to pick on people who might look different. Ask the children to think of something different about themselves – some children might need help with this; take care to be sensitive and emphasise why difference is a positive thing.

▶ Make clay cygnets using self-hardening grey clay with grey feathers pressed into them.

▶ Look at pictures of different baby farmyard birds, e.g. ducklings, chicken/pheasant/quail chicks, cygnets, goslings, poults (turkeys) and find similarities and differences.

▶ Make cut and stick pictures matching baby farm animals to parents.

▶ Have a small world farmyard pond with toy birds.

▶ Visit a local pond and feed the birds.

▶ Blow out eggshells and decorate them.

## Songs, rhymes and poems

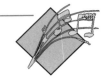

Five Little Ducks by Ian Beck – a traditional counting rhyme published as a picture book by Orchard Books.

Ugly Duckling by Danny Kaye – Find the lyrics to this song at www.angelfire.com/film/dannykaye/UglyDuckling.htm.

Little Duck – (Start with a Song: 70 Songs for the Early Years by Mavis de Mierre, Brilliant Publications.)

## Investigation area

Spot the odd one out:

1.  Put out some laminated pictures of groups of baby animals with one slightly different animal in each picture for children to find.
2.  Display a range of spot-the-difference pictures in the background.

## Alternate versions to the original tale

The Sissy Duckling by Harvey Fierstein & Henry Cole – a little duckling finds out that being different isn't all that bad.

The Very Ugly Bug by Liz Pinchon – an ugly little bug cannot camouflage himself like the other bugs.

Dilly Duckling by Claire Freedman & Jane Chapman – a little duckling chases after her lost feather.

Duck by Louise Spilsbury – information book about the life cycle of a duck.

Animal Babies on the Farm by Kingfisher – Pictures of farm animals with their young.

## Links with the EYFS Areas of Learning and Development

**PSED:** Have an awareness and pride in self as having own identity and abilities.

**KUW:** Find out about and identify some features of living things; investigate different meats and eggs; look closely at similarities, differences, patterns and change.

**PD:** Explore malleable materials; handle scissors safely and with increasing control.

**CD:** Create clay models; understand that different media can be combined to create new effects; work creatively on a small scale; explore colour and form in three dimensions.

# Stone Soup

Origin – Brothers Grimm
Moral – Everyone benefits from working together and sharing

## Activities to follow up the story

▶ Discuss the story – Ask the children to consider the actions of
the villagers when the travellers needed help; discuss the benefits
of kindness and sharing.

▶ Set the children a challenge that can only be achieved through group work
and collaboration, e.g. large-scale construction, tricky puzzles, a difficult
obstacle course.

▶ Visit a natural water source, e.g. stream, seaside, river, and collect some stones;
examine them and discuss how they have been smoothed by water over time;
compare to other rougher stones found in a park, garden or woodland area.

▶ Compare the weights of a variety of stones and rocks; use bucket scales to
find the heaviest; introduce standard weights for children to experiment with.

▶ Count, sort and classify different stones.

▶ Find out about the uses of different kinds of stone; learn about how it is
quarried and look at the machinery used to do this.

▶ Make some edible soup.

▶ Display some pictures of rock carvings in the art area for inspiration.

## Songs, rhymes and poems

Cooking Stone Soup at www.101kidz.com/poems/food.html

Under a Stone – rhyme (This Little Puffin, by Puffin Books)

Tasty Poems by Jill Bennett & Nick Sharratt – a selection of food poems (Oxford University Press)

## Investigation area

Strange soups:

1. Set up a big saucepan or cooking pot with wooden spoons; put out some unusual ingredients, e.g. toy bugs, cotton reels, leaves, pinecones, string, etc for children to make strange soups.
2. Provide recipe cards with strange but simple ingredient lists for children to read and create soups.
3. Provide blank recipe cards and pencils for children to make up their own strange soups.
4. Display a variety of soup cookery books and the children's recipe cards.

### Alternate versions to the original tale

Stone Soup by John W. Stewig & Margot Tomes – in this version a little girl tricks the stingy villagers.

Stone Soup by Jon J. Muth – the original story featuring three Chinese monks.

The Real Story of Stone Soup by Ying Chang Compestine & Stephanie Jorisch – Chinese story about three fishermen who trick their boss.

Pumpkin Soup by Helen Cooper – classic story about friendship.

Roald Dahl's Completely Revolting Recipes by Roald Dahl & Quentin Blake – some unusual ideas for cooking.

## Links with the EYFS Areas of Learning and Development

**PSED:** Learn social skills and enjoy being with and talking to adults and other children; work as part of a group or a class, sharing fairly; show care and concern for others; begin to recognise danger and know who to turn to for help.

**PSRN:** Order two items by weight; count reliably up to ten everyday objects; sort familiar objects to identify their similarities and differences, making choices and justifying decisions.

**KUW:** Investigate objects and materials by using all of their senses as appropriate; ask questions about why things happen and how things work.

# The Emperor's New Clothes

Origin – Hans Christian Anderson   Moral – Vanity could be your downfall

## Activities to follow up the story

▶ Discuss the story – talk about how the tailors were able to fool the emperor. Ask the children why they think the emperor believed the tailors.

▶ Design some clothes that are fit for an emperor; provide cardboard emperor templates and a variety of fabrics for the children to cut and stick on the template.

▶ Role-play tailors: provide a full-length mirror, a range of dressing up clothes and some measuring tapes.

▶ Provide clothing catalogues in the art area for cutting and sticking. Examine different types of clothing and decide where, why and for what purpose the items might be worn.

▶ Play a miming game – children take turns to mime putting on various items of clothing and everyone else has to guess what the items are.

▶ Adapt the above game by asking children to verbally describe where/how different items of clothing are worn.

▶ Look closely at a variety of patterned fabrics; ask children to describe the colours and shapes used in the patterns; challenge children to recreate the patterns either onto paper using paints/felt pens or onto fabric using paints/crayons.

## Songs, rhymes and poems

The Emperor's New Clothes – by Roald Dahl (Rhyme Stew, Puffin Books)

This is the Way We Wash Our Clothes – song (This Little Puffin, Puffin Books)

If Your Clothes Have Any Colour – poem at www.canteach.ca/elementary/songs-poems97.html

## Investigation area

Fit for an emperor:

1. Set out some fuzzy felt cards with emperor outlines on them and provide a variety of felt clothes for the children to create different looks.
2. Put out some buttons and coloured containers for children to sort by size, shape and colour.
3. Display the collaged fabric clothing designs made by the children.

### Alternate versions to the original tale

The Emperor's New Clothes by Alison Jay – with colourful illustrations.

The Emperor's New Underwear by Laurence Anholt & Arthur Robins – from the Seriously Silly Stories series.

Lulu's Clothes by Camilla Reid & Ailie Busby – novelty book that the children can interact with.

The Man Who Wore All His Clothes by Alan Ahlberg & Katherine McEwan – humorous story with great illustrations.

## Links with the EYFS Areas of Learning and Development

**PSED:** Have a sense of personal identity; express feelings in appropriate ways.

**CLL:** Use intonation, rhythm and phrasing to make their meaning clear to others; use a widening range of words to express or elaborate on ideas; sustain attentive listening, responding to what they have heard with relevant comments or questions.

**PSRN:** Talk about, recognise and recreate simple patterns.

**KUW:** Investigate objects and materials by using all of their senses as appropriate.

**CD:** Express and communicate their ideas by using a widening range of materials, designing and making; engage in imaginative play and role-play based on own first-hand experiences.

# The Leopard's Drum

Origin – Ghana     Moral – Appearances can be deceptive

## Activities to follow up the story

▶ Circle time – talk about difference. We all look different and have strengths in different areas, which may surprise others. Ask children to highlight their strengths.

▶ Use the story as a starting point for talking about sharing.

▶ Find examples of African tribal masks at www.afrikboutik.com or www.masksoftheworld.com and use these to inspire the children to make their own; use information books to find out what these masks mean and how tribes use them.

▶ Challenge the children to make a drum; investigate different materials for making drums of different shapes and strengths to produce a variety of sounds.

▶ Find out about tortoises; make tortoise shells by using cut up egg boxes to print rough circular shapes on sugar paper.

▶ Make pictures of jungle animals; cut out animal body parts in colourful tissue paper and create collages of animals.

▶ Play music in the outdoor area and put out a variety of everyday objects (pots, pans, tubs, tins) with different utensils (wooden and metal spoons, rulers, plastic hammers) for children to drum on.

▶ Role-play jungle: ask the children to help paint corrugated card for tree trunks, cut strips of crêpe paper for hanging vines and cut out sugar paper leaves.

▶ Small world jungle set up outside amongst some shrubbery or pot plants with toy animals.

## Songs, rhymes and poems

I am the Music Man – traditional rhyme retold in a picture book by Debra Potter (Child's Play)

The Leopard Who Lost His Spot by G. Porter, Hilda Offen, Esme Eve, Alan Jesset and Richard Hooke – poem at www.4to40.com/poems

Aiken Drum – find music and lyrics for this traditional song at www.songsforteaching.com

## Investigation area

Bang the drum:

1. Display an assortment of drums, e.g. bass, bongo, snare, tom-tom drums for children to compare designs and resulting sounds.
2. Display pictures of various drums being played by different types of musicians.
3. Set up a listening centre with headphones for children to listen to drum music of ranging tempos.

### Alternate versions to the original tale

How the Leopard Got His Spots by Rudyard Kipling – this traditional tale can be found in most collections of Kipling's stories.

Rumble in the Jungle by Giles Andreae & David Wojtowycz – a fun and colourful picture book full of wild animal rhymes.

Cockadoodle-doo, Mr Sultana! by Michael Morpurgo & Holly Swain – in this alternative story a rooster outwits a Sultan who is after a diamond.

## Links with the EYFS Areas of Learning and Development

**PSED:** Learn that they are special through the responses of adults to individual differences and similarities; have a positive self-image and show that they are comfortable with themselves; begin to learn that some things are shared.

**KUW:** Investigate objects and materials by using all of their senses as appropriate; ask questions about why things happen and how things work; begin to know about the cultures and beliefs of other people; construct with a wide range of objects, selecting appropriate resources and adapting work where necessary.

**PD:** Respond to rhythm and music by means of gesture and movement; show increasing control in holding and using beaters.

**CD:** Create collages; work creatively on a large scale; express themselves through physical action and sound.

# Goldilocks and the Three Bears

Origin – Victorian English   Moral – Do not wander off alone to explore strange places

## Activities to follow up the story

▶ Discuss the story – ask the children to consider what happened to Goldilocks when she wandered into a strange house; use the story to lead onto discussion about staying close to parents when out shopping etc.

▶ Make porridge; mix it into different consistencies (runny, thick, lumpy); add different flavourings (honey, jam, sugar); taste and compare.

▶ Compare and arrange small, medium and large sized objects by size.

▶ Compare quantities of liquids that will fit into small, medium and large bottles and jugs.

▶ Role-play the three bears' house.

▶ Have a teddy bears picnic outside; use different sized food, crockery and cutlery for children, adults and teddy bears.

▶ Make fierce bear masks!

▶ Visit some woods or go on a woodland trail – instruct the children to collect specific items, e.g. leaves, twigs, pinecones and conkers.

▶ Make a large-scale collage of the Three Bears with the woodland items.

## Songs, rhymes and poems

Bear by A.A. Milne (Elephants and Emus and Other Animal Rhymes, Philippa-Alys Browne)

When Goldilocks went to the house of the bears (Okki-tokki-unga: Action Rhymes for Children, A&C Black)

My Teddy Bear by Robin Mellor (Early Years Poems and Rhymes, Scholastic)

## Investigation area

Who's been eating my porridge?

1. Put small, medium and large bears on display; provide different sized objects for the children to match to each bear.
2. Set out some 'Compare Bears' and accompanying pattern cards (available from Amazon.co.uk).
3. Display different picture book versions and story posters.

### Alternate versions to the original tale

Goldilocks and the Three Bears by Niki Davies – story, songs and CD from Out of the Ark Music.

Mr Wolf and the Three Bears by Jan Fearnley – Mr Wolf plans a party for Baby Bear only to have it spoiled by Goldilocks.

Goldilocks by Stephen Tucker & Nick Sharratt – the story told in verse with modern illustrations and lift-the-flap.

Goldilocks Returns by Lisa Campbell Ernst – Goldilocks returns to visit the Three Bears as an adult.

In the Dark Dark Wood by Jessica Souhami – lift the flap book.

## Links with the EYFS Areas of Learning and Development

PSED: Begin to recognise danger and know who to turn to for help; be confident to try different types of porridge; express likes and dislikes.

PSRN: Begin to categorise objects according to size; order two items by capacity.

KUW: Investigate food, objects and materials by using all of their senses as appropriate; ask questions about why things happen and how things work.

CD: Work creatively on a large scale; create collages and masks; understand that different media can be combined to create new effects.

# The Little Match Girl

Origin – Hans Christian Anderson
Moral – Look after those less fortunate

## Activities to follow up the story

▶ Talk about poverty and homelessness. Ask the children to try and imagine how the Little Match Girl must be feeling while alone and cold outside; ask the children to think about what makes them feel cosy and safe at home. (Take care to be sensitive to the children's individual home situations.)

▶ Talk about fire saftey and consider the dangers of playing with matches.

▶ Put together some care packages for a local homeless charity such as The Salvation Army; collect non-perishable foods, toiletries and other essentials; ask the children to make cards and decorate the parcels.

▶ Provide some ready burned matchsticks for drawing pictures; put out some charcoals for additional use and comparison.

▶ Small world dolls' house.

## Songs, rhymes and poems

Cold Weather (This Little Puffin, Puffin Books)

Cold by Shirley Hughes (Olly and Me Out and About, Walker Books)

Star Light (Michael Foreman's Nursery Rhymes, Walker Books)

## Investigation area

How many matchsticks?

Set up an estimation game.

1. Drop some matchsticks into jars (safe matchsticks can be ordered from www.tts-group.co.uk).

2. Provide some paper and pencils for children to write down their name and guess at how many matchsticks there are in each jar; announce the closest estimations at the end of each day and change the amounts for the next day.

### Alternate versions to the original tale

The Little Match Girl by Jerry Pinkney & Hans Christian Andersen – the Picture Puffin version with beautiful illustrations.

Christmas Makes Me Think by Tony Medina & Chandra Cox – a little boy who is excited about Christmas takes some time to consider those less fortunate than him.

The Teddy Bear by David M. McPhail – touches on the issue of homelessness.

I Miss You: A First Look at Death by Pat Thomas – an early introduction to the subject of death.

Granpa by John Burningham – deals with death and loss in a subtle and sensitive way.

Disney/Pixar animation – find a beautiful animation of the tale at www.youtube.com/watch?v=yUSzQBaWq0Q

## Links with the EYFS Areas of Learning and Development

**PSED:** Show a strong sense of self as a member of different communities, such as their neighbourhood or family; show care and concern for others; feel safe and secure within healthy relationships with key people; begin to recognise danger and know who to turn to for help.

**KUW:** Ask questions about why things happen and how things work; develop an understanding of growth and decay over time; feel a sense of belonging to own community and place.

**CD:** Create matchstick pictures; create charcoal pictures.

# The Little Red Hen

Origin – Russian    Moral – There are benefits to helping others

## Activities to follow up the story

▶ Discuss the story – consider why the hen did not share her bread with the other animals. Discuss the benefits of helping others – talk about how it makes us feel as well as other possible rewards.

▶ Taste and compare different types of bread (white, crusty, wholemeal, brown, granary, flavoured).

▶ Bake bread; make loaves, buns and rolls of different shapes and sizes; try baking some without yeast and observe what happens.

▶ Visit a local bakery or role-play a bakery.

▶ Make a digital information book about the whole bread making process, from harvesting the wheat to baking the loaf. (Use a computer program such as Textease, PowerPoint or Smart Notebook.)

▶ Provide baking themed playdough resources.

▶ Learn about the life cycle of the chicken; set up an incubator in the setting and raise some chicks from eggs.

## Songs, rhymes and poems

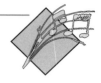

Slice, Slice, The Bread Looks Nice (This Little Puffin, Puffin Books)

Chook, Chook (A Child's Treasury of Nursery Rhymes, Kingfisher Books)

Making Bread www.parentinghumor.com/activityecenter/songsrhymes/makingbread.htm

## Investigation area

1. Set up a rotating cardboard wheel, divided into sections showing pictures from the story (hen planting the grains, watering them, harvesting the wheat, taking it to the mill, baking the bread).
2. Stick real-life representations of the same process around the outside of the wheel for children to match up.
3. Display bread-making ingredients, packaging and utensils.

---

### Alternate versions to the original tale

The Little Red Hen by Paul Galdone – includes an audio CD.

The Little Red Hen Makes a Pizza by Philemon Sturges & Amy Walrod – based on the original premise.

The Little Red Hen: A Deliciously Funny Flap Book by Jonathan Allen – lift the flap book.

From Wheat to Bread by Kristin Thoennes keller – 'From Farm to Table' information book for young children.

Baking Bread with Children by Warren Lee Cohen & Marije Rowling – contains recipes, stories, songs and poems.

---

## Links with the EYFS Areas of Learning and Development

**PSED:** Show care and concern for others; become more aware that choices have consequences; express likes/dislikes.

**CLL:** Show an understanding of how information can be found in non-fiction texts; attempt writing for different purposes.

**KUW:** Investigate objects and materials by using all of their senses as appropriate; describe and talk about what they see; show understanding of cause/effect relations; find out about, and identify some features of living things and events they observe; use ICT to support their learning.

# Puss in Boots

Origin - France    Moral – Work hard and achieve all you can

## Activities to follow up the story

▶ Set up scenarios using puppets to explore the issue of telling lies. Ask the children what they think about Puss' dishonesty; does it always turn out well for people who lie?

▶ Discuss the story in relation to the issues covered above – consider how Puss gained so much for his master; how can we achieve the most for ourselves? Consider the virtues of hard work.

▶ Ask the children to bring in a pair of wellington boots to be decorated with waterproof pens and paint.

▶ Find out about cats – wild and domestic. Ask children to bring in photos of their pet cats and to tell everyone about them.

▶ Follow my boots – help children make some boot prints using paint; cut out and laminate the prints; show children how to lay down boot trails around the setting (indoors and outside) for others to follow to find hidden objects. Incorporate the use of directional/positional language.

▶ Small world castle with princes, princesses, kings and queens.

▶ Look at some pictures of ogres; make ugly ogre masks.

## Songs, rhymes and poems

Cat in the Dark by Margaret Mahy (The Hutchinson Treasury of Children's Poetry)

Pussy Pussy Puddle Cat by Roger McGough (Sky in the Pie, Kestrel Books)

The Owl and the Pussycat by Edward Lear & Ian Beck (Corgi Children's Books)

## Investigation area

Booty:
1. Collect a selection of pairs of boots in different styles, shapes and sizes for a matching game.
2. Provide some labels for the boots (e.g. wellington, hiking, ankle, walking, riding, cowboy, dress, football, ski) for children to match to the boots.
3. Display pictures of people wearing these different styles of boots.

### Alternate versions to the original tale

Puss in Boots by Jess Stockham – lift the flap version with CD.

Puss in Boots (Play Along) by Adam Clay – board book with CD-ROM, audio version, games and puzzles.

King Pom and the Fox by Jessica Souhami – a Chinese version of Puss in Boots.

The Enchanted Gazelle and also Puss in Boots by Saviour Pirotta & Alan Marks – features an African fairy tale that is very similar to Puss in Boots, which is also included.

Storynory website – for a free audio version of the story go to http://storynory. com/2007/09/10/puss-in-boots/

## Links with the EYFS Areas of Learning and Development

PSED: Continue to be interested, excited and motivated to learn; understand what is right, what is wrong, and why; consider the consequences of their words and actions for themselves and others.

CLL: Speak clearly and audibly with confidence and control and show awareness of the listener.

PSRN: Use everyday words to describe position.

KUW: Find out about and identify some features of living things.

PD: Negotiate an appropriate pathway when setting down a boot trail both indoors and outdoors.

CD: Create painted patterns on boots; engage in imaginative and role-play.

# The Three Billy Goats Gruff

Origin - Norway   Moral – Be grateful for what you have

## Activities to follow up the story

▶ Discuss the story – consider how the troll is defeated because he is too greedy and makes the mistake of waiting for the biggest, fiercest billy goat.

▶ Display pictures and photographs of bridges from around the world in the construction area as inspiration.

▶ Challenge the children to build a strong, safe bridge using large wooden building blocks in the outdoor area.

▶ Taste some goat's milk, cheese and yogurt – compare with cow's milk products. (Ensure you check for allergies first.)

▶ Experiment with growing different types of grass and compare the results.

▶ Use a strong, sturdy table as a bridge and guide the children to act out the story.

▶ Use the 'trip trapping' sound of the goats as a starting point to think of how different animals might sound crossing the bridge; create a display of different animals painted by the children crossing a bridge, labelled with different sound words.

▶ Ask the children to help you set up a variety of balance beams and benches using PE apparatus; challenge the children to think of different ways to cross the benches and beams safely.

## Songs, rhymes and poems

London Bridge (Michael Foreman's Nursery Rhymes, Walker Books)

The Three Billy Goats Gruff – from Ros Bayley's Almost Traditional Tales series (Lawrence Educational). The story is told with rhyming raps incorporated into it.

## Investigation area

Who's that trip trapping over my bridge?

1. Set up a small bridge on a table, or the floor, and a range of toy animals in sets of three.
2. Challenge children to act out the story with the different sets of animals, making the appropriate sound for the different animal's footfalls.
3. Display pictures of different animals in the background.

### Alternate versions to the original tale

A Tale of Two Goats by Tom Barber & Rosalind Beardshaw – about a friendship between two goats from neighbouring farms.

The Troll by Julia Donaldson – a troll wants goat for dinner but has to make do with fish instead.

Giddy Goat by Jamie Rix & Lynne Chapman – the story of a mountain goat who is scared of heights.

The Three Billy Goats' Stuff! by Bob Hartman & Jacqueline East – a twist on the original story about a bullying troll.

Little Apple Goat by Caroline Jayne Church – about a little goat who likes to eat fruit.

## Links with the EYFS Areas of Learning and Development

PSED: Continue to be interested, excited and motivated to learn; understand what is right, what is wrong, and why; consider the consequences of their words and actions for themselves and others.

CLL: Speak clearly and audibly with confidence and control and show awareness of the listener.

PSRN: Use everyday words to describe position.

KUW: Find out about and identify some features of living things.

PD: Negotiate an appropriate pathway when setting down a boot trail both indoors and outdoors.

CD: Create painted patterns on boots; engage in imaginative and role-play.

# Snow White and the Seven Dwarfs

Origin – the Brothers Grimm
Moral – We cannot always have everything we want

## Activities to follow up the story

▶ Discuss the story – talk about feelings of envy and jealousy; make analogies at the children's level, e.g. wanting toys that other children have.

▶ Circle time – talk about what happened to Snow White when she accepted the apple from the old woman. Discuss 'stranger danger'.

▶ Make an apple pie, apple crumble or stuffed baked apples.

▶ Find out about different types of apples – taste them and compare.

▶ Paint self-portraits using mirrors; help the children mix colours to match their eye, hair and skin colours.

▶ Talk about how we feel at different times and on different occasions; talk about the seven dwarfs' different personalities and discuss how they express their feelings; consider how we deal with the different feelings we experience.

▶ Make mood hats: cut out dwarf hat card templates labelled with each of the seven dwarf's names; challenge the children to decorate each hat to reflect the mood and personality of each dwarf.

44

## Songs, rhymes and poems

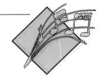

Snow White and the Seven Dwarfs by Roald Dahl (Revolting Rhymes, Puffin Books)

I've Got a Basket of Apples by Elizabeth Matterson et al (This Little Puffin, Puffin Books)

Heigh Ho – song featured in the Disney film clip at www.youtube.com/watch?v=aURThUaRjCc&NR=1

## Investigation area

How do you feel today?

1. Put a mirror up and stick some pictures of people making different facial expressions around it.
2. Label the faces according to the feeling they are depicting.
3. Display some open questions as prompts, e.g. How do you feel today? How does it make you feel when...? What makes you feel happy/sad/angry? What does it feel like to be in a good/bad mood?

### Alternate versions to the original tale

Snow White by Jane Ray – an unusual book with just six pages; the story is told using six 3D peep-through tableaux.

Snow White and the Seven Aliens by Laurence Anholt & Arthur Robins – from the Seriously Silly Stories series.

Snow White in New York by Fiona French – set in the 1920s with jazz musicians as dwarfs.

Apples by Louise Spilsbury – information book for children.

## Links with the EYFS Areas of Learning and Development

PSED: Express their feelings within warm, mutual, affirmative relationships; express feeling in appropriate ways; begin to recognise danger and know who to turn to for help.

CLL: Use a widening range of words to express ideas; use language as a powerful means of sharing feelings, experiences and thoughts.

KUW: Investigate objects using all of their senses as appropriate; look closely at similarities and differences.

CD: Create paintings; explore what happens when they mix colours; choose particular colours to use for a purpose; express and communicate feelings by using a widening range of materials.

# The Musicians of Bremen

Origin – the Brothers Grimm   Moral – The elderly must be cared for and respected

## Activities to follow up the story

▶ Discuss the story – think about what happens to people and animals as they get older; help the children to understand that life can become more difficult.

▶ Circle time – talk about elderly relatives.

▶ Make Christmas cards for the elderly people living in a local residential home.

▶ Play a variety of music in the setting; talk about the different genres; ask the children to express their likes/dislikes of different types; ask the children how different music makes them feel. (Try to find some scary music to help the children understand how the robbers felt.)

▶ Do some freestyle painting in time to music.

▶ Play a listening game – sit some children in a line with one child blindfolded out at the front; one child in the line shakes a tambourine and the child at the front must guess which direction the sound came from and who it might have been.

▶ Invite a professional musician into the setting to do a workshop.

▶ Go and see a big band.

▶ Bang different numbers of beats on a drum; ask children to close their eyes and count beats.

46

## Songs, rhymes and poems

Schlaf, Kindlein, Schlaf – a German lullaby (Skip Across the Ocean, Frances Lincoln)

I am the Music Man by Debra Potter (Child's Play)

Hey Diddle Diddle (Michael Foreman's Nursery Rhymes, Walker Books)

## Investigation area

What am I playing?
1. Set up a table with a divide across the middle to block the view.
2. Set out some pairs of musical instruments – one on each side of the divide for the children to play the instruments to each other and guess what they are. Provide written labels to be displayed next to each instrument.
3. Display pictures of instruments, orchestras and examples of music scores.

### Alternate versions to the original tale

The Musicians of Bremen by Susanna Davidson & Mike Gordon – the original story with lively modern illustrations.

The Bremen Town Musicians by Jacob Grimm, Wilhelm Grimm, Bernadette Watts & Anthea Bell – the classic story retold.

The Bremen Town Musicians: Grimm's Fairy Tale illustrated by Lai Hsin-Shih – featuring beautiful illustrations.

Musical Instruments by Claude Delafosse, Gallimard Jeunesse & Donald Grant – information book for young children.

Tonight's Bedtime Story website – find an outline of this story and others at www.tonightsbedtimestory.com/the-bremen-town-musicians/

## Links with the EYFS Areas of Learning and Development

PSED: Show a strong sense of self as a member of different communities, such as their neighbourhood or family; show care and concern for others; express likes/dislikes.

CLL: Distinguish one musical sound from another; show interest in play with musical sounds.

PSRN: Count actions that cannot be moved.

CD: Begin to use representation as a form of communication; respond in a variety of ways to what they hear; show an interest in the way musical instruments sound; explore the different sounds of instruments.

# Singing to the Sun

Origin – Modern day fairy tale by Vivian French
Moral – There is wealth in happiness

## Activities to follow up the story

▶ Talk about the story – ask the children why they think Prince Thorfinn chooses happiness rather than wealth or power.

▶ Circle time – talk about what makes us feel happy.

▶ Use puppets to explore the issues raised in the story and set up scenarios that involve: puppets hogging all the toys and refusing to share but playing alone as a consequence; puppets bossing others about and alienating others as a result; puppets playing together, sharing and cooperating and making friends.

▶ Discuss the 'surprise' ending; ask the children how they feel about how the story ends; ask the children to make some suggestions for alternatives that they would prefer.

▶ Find out what a court jester does.

▶ Role-play a castle with king, queen, prince, princess and jester costumes.

▶ Small world fairy tale land (find an Active World fairy tale mat at www.tts-group.co.uk).

▶ Make royal bejewelled crowns using a variety of craft materials.

## Songs, rhymes and poems

If You're Happy and You Know It by Jan Omerod & Lindsey Gardiner
– a rhyme in picture book form (Oxford University Press)

As I Was Walking Down the Street – action song (This Little Puffin, Puffin Books)

Greedy by Felicia Law (Feelings: A First Poem Book About Feelings, Mercury Books)

## Investigation area

All in jest:

1. Set up a joke corner with some comfy chairs.
2. Ask the children to bring in jokes from home. Provide a decorated, colourful, sparkly shoe box with a slot in the top for collecting them.
3. Pick jokes out of the box to read to children who visit the corner and encourage children to make up their own jokes.
4. Display pictures of jesters and some jokes on the wall and put out joke books for young children.

### Alternate versions to the original tale

Evil Weasel by Hannah Shaw – a greedy little weasel is very rich but has no friends because he is so mean.

The King of Capri by Jeanette Winterson & Jane Ray – a greedy king learns about the virtues of generosity.

Happy! by Caroline Castle and Sam Childs – Little Zeb book about feeling happy.

The Ha Ha Bonk Book by Janet & Allan Ahlberg – illustrated joke book for children.

My Very First Joke Book by Kaye Umansky – jokes for younger children.

## Links with the EYFS Areas of Learning and Development

**PSED:** Have an awareness and pride in self; form friendships with other children; become aware that choices have consequences; express feelings.

**CLL:** Listen with enjoyment and respond to stories; suggest how the story might end.

**CD:** Use ideas involving fitting and overlapping; choose colours for a particular purpose; use their imagination in art and design, imaginative and role-play.

# The Little Mermaid

Origin – Hans Christian Anderson   Moral – Listen to and respect your parents

## Activities to follow up the story

▶ Talk about the story – ask the children to consider what happens to the Little Mermaid when she disregards her parents' wishes.

▶ Make a collage of mermaid pictures: cut coloured cellophane and tissue paper into the shape of scales and stick onto mermaid templates. Or make shell collages.

▶ Role-play a beach house.

▶ Practise fine motor movements using shallow trays of wet and dry sand and a variety of mark-making tools. Make repeating patterns with shells. Decorate pebbles with acrylic paints.

▶ Small world sea life and 'merpeople' in the water tray.

▶ Make mermaid charms by threading shiny, glittery shells or beads onto string.

▶ Bury shells in the sand tray; give children verbal descriptions of different shells and ask them to find the right ones.

## Songs, rhymes and poems

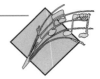

Seaside by Shirley Hughes – poem (Olly and Me Out and About, Walker Books)

Seaside Poems by Jill Bennett & Nick Sharratt (A collection of illustrated poems, Oxford University Press)

Mermaid Poems by Clare Bevan (Macmillan)

## Investigation area

Oh I do like to be beside the seaside:

1. Create a lift-the-flap seaside game – stick pictures of seaside items on a display board underneath shell-shaped flaps.
2. Set out some alphabet cards with Velcro on the back and challenge the children to match the initial sounds to the pictures.
3. Differentiate by setting out some cards with the whole words on them.

---

### Alternate versions to the original tale

Can You Catch a Mermaid by Jane Ray – a fisherman's daughter finds friendship with a mermaid.

Dear Mermaid by Alan Durant & Vanessa Cabban – a little girl meets a mermaid while on holiday.

The Tiniest Mermaid – a little girl rescues a little mermaid from a storm and nurses her back to health.

Magic Beach by Alison Lester – picture book about a magical day at the beach – full of imagery and rhyme.

Disney's Little Mermaid – find the animated film version of this story on DVD at www.amazon.co.uk

---

## Links with the EYFS Areas of Learning and Development

PSED: Have an awareness of boundaries; understand; consider the consequences of their actions for themselves and others.

PSRN: Talk about and create simple patterns.

KUW: Investigate objects and materials by using all of their senses as appropriate; explore and play with sand.

PD: Engage in activities that requiring hand-eye coordination; show increasing control in holding and using mark-making tools.

CD: Create collages; create and experiment with colour and marks; begin to make-believe by pretending.

# The Ant and the Grasshopper

Origin – Aesop's fable   Moral – Hard work reaps reward

## Activities to follow up the story

► Discuss the story – ask the children why the grasshopper ended up hungry when winter came. Consider the dilemma as to whether it was fair of the ant to refuse to help the grasshopper.

► Look at how different foods are stored: find out about tinned and dried foods, compare them to refrigerated foods, such as cheese and meat, as well as other perishables, such as fruit and vegetables.

► Leave some food to go mouldy – observe what happens using a digital microscope and record the different stages of decay using a digital camera.

► Use toy ants to set up different number problems, e.g. finding which colony has the most/least ants; dividing a colony into groups; finding the total number of ants from two colonies.

► Set up a life size ant farm using climbing apparatus for children to climb up, down, through, over and under as if they were ants in the tunnels!

► Set up some low hurdles and obstacles for children to jump over like grasshoppers.

► Find out about how grasshoppers make the singing sounds with their legs; experiment with rubbing different objects together to make sounds.

## Songs, rhymes and poems

Ants Live Here by Lilian Moore (Hutchinson Treasury of Children's Poetry)

The Grasshopper and the Bird by James Reeves (the Oxford Treasury of Children's Poetry)

The Grasshopper and the Ants by G. Porter at www.4to40.com/poems/index.asp?id=283

## Investigation area

Ant farm:
1. Set up an ant farm (kit available from Amazon.co.uk).
2. Put out some magnifiers for the children to observe more closely.
3. Display information books about how ants live and work together in colonies.
4. Display some close up photographs of worker ants marching in trails.

## Alternate versions to the original tale

Who's Got Game? by Toni Morrison, Slade Morrison & Pascal Lemaitre – a modern version of the original fable with a twist.

The Ants Go Marching by Dan Crisp – a great picture book that aims to improve observations skills and incorporates a bit of maths.

Find Anthony Ant by Laura Philpot & Graham Philpot – an activity book full of rhymes, mazes and number challenges.

One Hundred Hungry Ants by Elino J. Pinczes – a group of ants get distracted on their way to a picnic.

The Three Grasshoppers by Francesca Bosca & Giuliano Ferri – three grasshoppers must work together to prepare for winter.

## Links with the EYFS Areas of Learning and Development

PSED: Have a positive approach to activities; show care and concern for others.

PSRN: In practical activities and discussion, begin to use the vocabulary involved in adding and subtracting; use developing mathematical ideas and methods to solve practical problems.

KUW: Describe and talk about what they see; show understanding of cause/effect relations; show an awareness of change; show curiosity about why things happen and how things work.

PD: Travel around, under, over and through balancing and climbing equipment; move freely with pleasure and confidence; show awareness of food hygiene.

CD: Create sounds by rubbing objects together.

# Mama Panya's Pancakes

Origin – Kenyan village tale    Moral – Kindness is rewarded

## Activities to follow up the story

▶ Discuss the story – ask the children if they understand why Mama Panya was worried about how many people Adika was inviting. Do the children understand why everything turned out fine in the end? Talk about kindness and sharing.

▶ Make pancakes: make sweet and savoury types and taste with different fillings. Make American style pancakes or French galettes.

▶ Create a pictogram to display which pancake filling is the most popular. (Use a computer program to do this such as 2Count.)

▶ Invite parents and siblings to the setting for a pancake party.

▶ Role-play a market outdoors. Role-play a pancake restaurant indoors or a role-play pancake stand outdoors.

▶ Play pancake number games: share pancakes out between children; decide how many more/less pancakes are needed; find out how many pancakes there are altogether, etc.

▶ Learn about the significance of Shrove Tuesday for Christians.

▶ Play a memory game – 'I ate pancakes for tea and on them I had...'

▶ Learn about life in Kenya.

## Songs, rhymes and poems

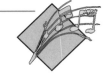

Mummy Made Pancakes on Tuesday by Shaun Fountain
(This Little Puffin, Puffin Books)

Mix a Pancake by Christina Rossetti at www.scrapbook.com/
poems/doc/3068/53.html

The Pancake Collector by Jack Prelutsky (One Hundred Years of Poetry for Children,
Oxford University Press)

## Investigation area

Enough for a little bit and a little bit more...

1. Set out some pancake ingredient packaging and price it with simple amounts,
   e.g. 1p, 2p, etc.
2. Provide some play coins and put out some laminated shopping lists for
   children to use and attempt to buy as many items as possible with the
   money provided.
3. Display photos of the children making their pancakes.

### Alternate versions to the original tale

Mr Wolf's Pancakes by Jan Fearnley – no one will help Mr Wolf make some
pancakes, but everyone wants to help him eat them.

Pancakes, Pancakes! by Eric Carle – details the stages of pancake making with
the trademark illustrations.

The Big Pancake by Ladybird – the traditional tale about a pancake that does
not want to be eaten.

## Links with the EYFS Areas of Learning and Development

**PSED:** Understand that their needs to be agreed values and codes of behaviour for
groups of people to work together harmoniously; show a strong sense of
self as a member of different communities, such as their family or setting;
understand that people have different cultures and beliefs that need to be
treated with respect.

**CLL:** Sustain attentive listening, responding to what they have heard with
relevant comments.

**PSRN:** Share objects into equal groups and count how many in each group; use
language such as 'more' or 'less' to compare two numbers; in practical
activities begin to use the vocabulary involved in adding.

**KUW:** Investigate objects and materials by using all of their senses as appropriate;
use ICT to support their learning.

# The Elves and the Shoemaker

Origin – the Brothers Grimm   Moral – One good turn deserves another

## Activities to follow up the story

▶ Discuss the story – ask the children why they think the elves wanted to help the shoemaker. Consider the idea that they did not expect anything in return but were rewarded anyway.

▶ Practise tying shoe laces – make it a focus skill for a week. Put out some thread and lace cards.

▶ Role-play a shoemakers: provide scraps of leather, canvas and PVC, toy hammers, scissors, pliers, a selection of old shoes, foot size measurer, dress-maker's tape measure and shoe boxes. Role-play a shoe shop.

▶ Print patterns using shoelaces dipped in paint.

▶ Find out everyone's shoe sizes and make comparisons – who has the biggest/ smallest feet?

▶ Find out how many footsteps it takes to travel to various areas in the setting.

## Songs, rhymes and poems

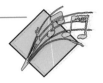

I Can Tie My Shoe Lace (Michael Foreman's Nursery Rhymes, Walker Books)

There was an Old Woman who Lived in a Shoe (Lavender's Blue, Oxford University Press)

The Little Elf by John K. Bangs at www.fairiesworld.com/fairypoems/elfpoem6.shtml

## Investigation area

Funny feet:
1. Set out 'Tie My Shoes' activities for children to practise on (available from the Early Learning Centre).
2. Create a wall display of paper cut outs of children's feet, named and arranged in size order.
3. Display questions such as, 'Who has the biggest feet?' 'Who needs size 4 shoes?' 'Which children have size 5 feet?'
4. Display some rhymes and poems about feet.

### Alternate versions to the original tale

The Elves and the Emperor by Hilary Robinson – from the Fairytale Jumbles series. Some elves help the Emperor make some new clothes.

The Elves Big Adventure by Daniela Drescher – some elves have an adventure in a hot air balloon.

Centipede's 100 shoes by Tony Ross – a fun counting book.

Lulu's Shoes by Camilla Reid & Ailie Busby – a touch and feel book for young children.

## Links with the EYFS Areas of Learning and Development

PSED: Consider the consequences of their words and actions for themselves and others; seek to do things for themselves, knowing that an adult is close by, ready to support if needed; dress and undress independently.

PSRN: Order items by size; count actions; count aloud in ones.

KUW: Show and awareness of change; investigate materials by using all of their senses as appropriate.

PD: Engage in activities requiring hand-eye coordination; show increasing control over clothing and fastenings.

CD: Begin to make-believe by pretending; engage in imaginative play and role-play; create printed paintings.

# Rapunzel

Origin – Brothers Grimm   Moral – It is wrong to steal from others

## Activities to follow up the story ──────────────

▶ Discuss the story – ask the children why the witch wanted to take Rapunzel from her family in the first place. Talk about why stealing is wrong.

▶ Pose the question, 'Is it stealing if...?' Present the children with different scenarios using puppets to explore what 'stealing' actually means.

▶ Play a memory game: put some items on a table, show them to the children and cover them with a sheet; use a hand puppet, e.g. fox or wolf to 'steal' an item and ask the children to guess what has gone missing.

▶ Role-play a hairdresser.

▶ Learn how to plait ribbons tied to railings.

▶ Make patterns by dragging pieces of rope across wet sand.

▶ Practise climbing ropes on purpose-built climbing apparatus.

▶ Compile a survey about everyone's hair in the setting; find out which children have different colours and lengths of hair; make some bar charts to display the results; ask questions about the results such as whether there are more/ less children with long/short, brown/blonde/black hair.

## Songs, rhymes and poems

Rapunzel! Rapunzel! by Kenn Nesbitt (My Hippo has the Hiccups and Other Poems I Totally Made Up, Sourcebooks)

Her Long Hair is Her Pillow (The Kingfisher Book of Children's Poetry)

Rapunzel by Kaye Umansky (Nonsense Fairytale Rhymes, Open University Press)

## Investigation area

The tallest tower:
1. Set aside a large space and provide a range of construction kits such as duplo/wooden bricks/lego/brio.
2. Challenge the children to find out which kit will build the tallest tower.
3. Display posters of tall buildings and information books about construction; provide a digital camera to take photos of the children's accomplishments – display these also.

### Alternate versions to the original tale

Rapunzel by John Kurtz – an African-American version of the story.

Rapunzel by Paul O. Zelinsky – Picture Puffin version with classic illustrations.

I Love My Hair by Natasha Anastasia – a little girl describes all the different ways she can wear her hair.

Crazy Hair Day by Barney Saltzberg – a little boy styles his hair for crazy hair day at school only to find out that he has got the wrong day.

Going to the Hairdresser: A Guide for Children with Autism and Asperger Syndrome by Laura Slade & Dennis Ayris – information book published by the National Autistic Society.

## Links with the EYFS Areas of Learning and Development

PSED: Understand what is right, what is wrong, and why.

PSRN: Count an irregular arrangement of objects; use language such as more or less to compare quantities.

KUW: Construct with a purpose in mind; investigate rope; notice and comment on patterns.

PD: Demonstrate increasing skill and control in the use of blocks and constructions sets; engage in activities requiring hand-eye coordination; manipulate materials to achieve a planned effect; climb up climbing equipment.

CD: Engage in imaginative and role-play based on own first-hand experiences.

# Hansel and Gretel

Origin – Brother Grimm    Moral – Beware of strangers

## Activities to follow up the story

▶ Discuss the story – ask the children if they think Hansel and Gretel did the right thing by trusting the old woman. Talk about getting lost and the type of people who are best to approach for help, e.g. police officers.

▶ Sort and make patterns with dolly mixtures or smarties.

▶ Make gingerbread houses and decorate with coloured icing and colourful sweets.

▶ Role-play a sweet shop or chocolatier; get the children to make toy sweets using salt-dough, paint them and wrap them in coloured cellophane; provide weighing scales.

▶ Lay down 'breadcrumb' trails for the children to follow.

▶ Talk about why sweets, chocolate and cake are foods that should be eaten in moderation and as part of a balanced diet and an active lifestyle.

▶ Create a large-scale board game with a number track path through some woods to a candy house and play giant dice games.

▶ Collect sweet papers and use them for creating collages.

## Songs, rhymes and poems

Hansel and Gretel by Roald Dahl (Rhyme Stew, Puffin Books)

Chocolate Cake by Michael Rosen – a long story-poem
at www.poemhunter.com/poem/chocolate-cake

Sweets and Treats by Bobbye S. Goldstein – a compilation of poems about sweets
and puddings (Hyperion Books)

## Investigation area

Sugar and spice and all things nice...

1. Set out a range of sweet food packaging – both healthy (fruits, yoghurts, honey) and unhealthy (sweets, chocolates, cakes).
2. Provide sorting hoops labelled 'healthy' and 'unhealthy' for the children to sort the packaging.
3. Display healthy eating posters and books.

### Alternate versions to the original tale

Hansel and Gretel by the Brothers Grimm & Rachel Isadora – the story retold in an African setting.

The Truth About Hansel and Gretel by Karina Law & Elke Counsell – told from the point of view of the old lady.

Chocolates and Sweets to Make by Rebecca Gilpin & Catherine Atkinson – recipes book.

CBeebies Something Special Stories – find an interactive electronic version of the story at
www.bbc.co.uk/cbeebies/somethingspecial/stories/hanselandgretel.html

## Links with the EYFS Areas of Learning and Development

PSED: Begin to recognise danger and know who to turn to for help; feel safe and secure within healthy relationships with key people; have a developing awareness of their own feelings.

CLL: Show an understanding of the elements of stories.

PSRN: Talk about and create patterns; use and say number names in order in familiar contexts.

PD: Show awareness of a range of healthy practices with regard to eating.

CD: Create collages; create decorated gingerbread houses; begin to make-believe by pretending.

# Anansi and the Boastful Bullfrog

Origin – Caribbean    Moral – Telling lies can hurt others

## Activities to follow up the story

▶ Discuss the story – ask the children to think about why Anansi told the lies he did; talk about how sometimes other people can be annoying and discuss possible best approaches to dealing with such people; look at the consequences of Anansi's lies for the bullfrog.

▶ Find out about bullfrogs using Internet CD-ROMs and information books.

▶ In music and movement sessions, jump like bullfrogs, crawl like lizards and scamper like spiders. Play bullfrog hopscotch.

▶ Collect some frogspawn and observe it as it changes.

▶ Make cut and stick life-cycle wheels about the frog.

▶ Discuss fear of spiders; ask the children how they feel about spiders and, if they are scared, what is it about them that makes them feel that way.

▶ Use the characters' Jamaican speech in the book as a starting point for talking about language, accent and dialect.

## Songs, rhymes and poems

Five Green and Speckled Frogs – a counting rhyme at
www.dltk-teach.com/rhymes/frogs/index.htm

I have a little spider (This Little Puffin, Puffin Books)

The Bullfrog Song at www.kidzone.ws/lw/frogs/activities-songs.htm.

## Investigation area

Incey wincey spider...

1. Set up a vivarium containing spiders – encourage the children to catch some and add to the collection.
2. Provide clipboards, paper and colouring pencils for the children to make observational drawings of the spiders.
3. Display some information books about spiders and posters with close-up images.

## Alternate versions to the original tale

Anansi the Spider by G. McDermot – useful picture book for introducing the character Anansi.

Aaarrgghh, Spider! by Lydia Monks – picture book exploring the common fear of spiders.

Spiders (Usborne Beginners) by Rebecca Gilpin – information book for young children.

British Council website – find the animated story of Why Anansi Has Thin Legs as well as printable flash cards to help tell and make up stories about the spider on the Internet at www.britishcouncil.org/kids-stories-anansi.htm

## Links with the EYFS Areas of Learning and Development

PSED: Learn social skills, and enjoy being with and talking to adults and other children; are aware that some actions can hurt or harm others; understand what is right, what is wrong, and why; express their feelings within warm, mutual, affirmative relationships.

CLL: Enjoy listening to and using spoken language.

PSRN: Use and say number names in order in familiar contexts.

KUW: Find out about and identify some features of living things; describe and talk about what they see; use ICT to support their learning.

PD: Move freely with pleasure and confidence in a range of ways, such as jumping, crawling and scampering.

# Rumpelstiltskin

Origin – Brothers Grimm    Moral – Do not brag and tell lies

## Activities to follow up the story

▶ Discuss the story – ask the children to consider what happened to the miller's daughter when he lied about her and she then continued the lie.

▶ Make name dictionaries: ask each child to think of five words that begin with the same letter as the initial sound in their name; make a mini booklet featuring this sound with drawn or cut and stick pictures.

▶ Write very simple acrostic poems using the children's names as starting points; ask the children to think of adjectives about themselves to match each letter in their name.

▶ Use Rumpelstiltskin as inspiration for creating strange little creatures with unusual names; look in some books at pictures of mythical characters; ask the children to paint or draw a character of their own and give it a name.

▶ Count the letters in children's names; find out who has the longest/shortest first name or surname or both together.

▶ Find out what kinds of materials are spun and how this is done.

## Songs, rhymes and poems

Rumpelstiltskin at www.landofnurseryrhymes.co.uk/htm_pages/Rumpelstiltskin.htm

Rumpelstiltskin by Kaye Umansky (Nonsense Fairytale Rhymes, Open University Press)

Wind the Bobbin Up (Playtime Rhymes for Little People, Barefoot Books)

## Investigation area

What's in a name?

1. Provide some phonix cubes for children to build their names or put out some letter stamps and ink for children to print their names.
2. Set out laminated name cards for children to trace over and practise writing their names.
3. Put out some objects for children to pick out as having matching initial sounds with their names.
4. Display the children's acrostic poems.

---

### Alternate versions to the original tale

Rumpelstiltskin (Graphic Spin) by Martin Powell & Erik Valdez Y. Alanis – comic book version of the story.

Guess My Name by Saviour Pirotta & Alan Marks – a Celtic fairy tale with a similar theme.

My Name is Not Isabella by Jennifer Fosberry – a little girl spends a day changing her name.

## Links with the EYFS Areas of Learning and Development

**PSED:** Are aware that some actions can hurt or harm others; understand what is right, what is wrong, and why.

**CLL:** Link sounds to letters; hear and say the initial sound in words and know which letters represent some of the sounds; use their phonic knowledge to write simple regular words and make phonetically plausible attempts at more complex words; use a widening range of words to express or elaborate on ideas.

**PSRN:** Count reliably up to ten everyday objects; use language such as 'more' or 'less' to compare two numbers.

**KUW:** Show curiosity about how things work.

**CD:** Express and communicate their ideas and thoughts by using a widening range of materials.

# The Sun and the Wind

Origin – Aesop's fable     Moral – A gentle approach is often best

## Activities to follow up the story

▶ Discuss the story – consider who was most successful, the sun or the wind; ask the children to explain why. Talk about why a gentle approach is often best, rather than being aggressive and shouting or hitting out.

▶ Fill water bomb balloons with runny yellow and orange paint and drop them from a height onto large pieces of blue poster paper to create sunshine splats (best done outdoors and with protective clothing on!).

▶ Put out sunshine coloured paints for the children to dip their hands into and print suns.  Do some blow painting.

▶ Make hand held windmills (find a template and instructions on the Met Office website at www.metoffice.gov.uk/education/kids/weather_experiments_wind mill.html).

▶ Race toy sailboats in the water tray, using hand held fans to push them along.

▶ Fly kites on a windy day.

▶ Go for a walk on a sunny/windy day and ask the children to describe how the weather feels; record these descriptions and display them on a weather or seasons display.

## Songs, rhymes and poems

Sunshine and Wind Song (Start with a Song: 70 Songs for the Early Years by Mavis De Mierre, Brilliant Publications)

Find a selection of songs about the wind and other weather at www.preschooleducation.com/sweather.shtml

## Investigation area

Clothing for all weathers...

1. Divide a table up into four sections and label them Winter, Summer, Spring and Autumn.
2. Stick pictures depicting the typical weather for each season in each section.
3. Provide a box of clothing and accessories that might be needed during each season for the children to sort into the sections.
4. Display weather pictures in the background.

### Alternate versions to the original tale

The North Wind and the Sun by Brian Wildsmith – with beautiful illustrations.

Sunshine by Jan Ormerod – wordless picture book.

Winnie the Pooh and the Blustery Day by Disney – Pooh Bear's adventures on a particularly windy day.

The Wind Blew by Pat Hutchins – picture book with rhyming verse.

One Windy Wednesday by Phyllis Root – the wind blows the voices out of some animals and mixes them up.

The Little Book of Outside in All Weathers by Sally Featherstone – lots of ideas for planning outdoor activities.

## Links with the EYFS Areas of Learning and Development

**PSED:** Express needs and feelings in appropriate ways; learn social skills, and enjoy being with and talking to adults and other children; contribute to own self-control.

**CLL:** Build up vocabulary that reflects the breadth of their experiences; link statements and stick to a main theme or intention; use language as a powerful means of sharing experiences and thoughts; use talk to explain what is happening.

**KUW:** Find out about and identify some features of weather events; ask questions about why things happen and how things work; begin to try out a range of tools and techniques safely.

**CD:** Create splatter paintings, blow paintings and printed paintings.

# Book List

Little Red Riding Hood – Nick Sharratt & Stephen Tucker
9780333962176, Macmillan

The Hare and the Tortoise – Brian Wildsmith
9780192727084, Oxford University Press

The Three Little Pigs – Susanna Davidson & George Overwater
9780746096529, Usborne Publishing

Lazy Lion – Mwenye Hadithi & Adrienne Kennaway
9780-440-0845-287, Hodder Children's Books

The Gingerbread Man – A. Macdonald & Anja Reiger
9780721497310, Ladybird Books

Thumbelina – Lucy M. George & Rachel Swirles
9781845393045, Meadowside Children's Books

Jack and the Beanstalk – Richard Walker & Niamh Sharkey
9781905236428, Barefoot Books

The Enormous Turnip – I. Yates & Ian Lewis
9780721497389, Ladybird Books

The Town Mouse and the Country Mouse – Susanna Davidson & Jacqueline East
9780746088579, Usborne Publishing

The Ugly Ducking – Ian Beck
9781846165801, Orchard Books

Stone Soup – Jess Stockham
9781846430213, Child's Play

The Emperor's New Clothes – Alison Edgson
9781846430206, Child's Play

The Leopard's Drum – Jessica Souhami
9781-84507-419-7, Frances Lincoln

Goldilocks and the Three Bears – Lauren Child & Emily Jenkins
9780141501253, Puffin Books

The Little Match Girl – Christine San Jose
9781590780008, Boyds Mills Press

The Little Red Hen – Byron Barton
9780064433792, Harper Collins

Puss in Boots – Margaret Mayo & Philip Norman
9781843624547, Orchard Books

The Three Billy Goats Gruff – Mary Finch & Roberta Arenson
9781846860720, Barefoot Books

Snow White and the Seven Dwarfs – Lesley Danson
9781846430237, Child's Play

The Bremen Town Musicians – Brothers Grimm, Lisbeth Zwerger & Anthea Bell
9780698400429, Putnam Publishing

Singing to the Sun – Vivian French & Jackie Morris
9781405227513, Egmont

The Little Mermaid – Hans Christian Anderson, Christian Birmingham
9781406317909, Walker Books

The Ant and the Grasshopper – Amy Lowry Poole
9780823414772, Holiday House

Mama Panya's Pancakes – Mary & Rich Chamberlin & Julia Cairns
9781-905236-63-3, Barefoot Books

The Elves and the Shoemaker – Brothers Grimm & Jim LaMarche
9780811834773, Chronicle Books

Rapunzel: A Fairy Tale – Jacob Grimm, Wilhelm Grimm, Maja Dusikova & Anthea Bell
9780735813045, North-South Books

Hansel and Gretel – Anthony Browne
9781406318524, Walker Books

Anansi and Boastful Bullfrog – 'H' Patten & John Clementson
978-0-7112-1401-9, Frances Lincoln

Rumpelstiltskin – Ladybird
9781846469930, Ladybird Books

The Sun and the Wind – Aesop, Mairi MacKinnon & Francesca Di Chiara
9780746095836, Usborne

# Further reading
## Storybooks

The Rainbow Book of Nursery Tales
by Sam Childs

Revolting Rhymes
by Roald Dahl

Mixed Up Fairy Tales
by Hilary Robinson & Nick Sharratt

Fairy Tales and Fantastic Stories
by Terry Jones & Michael Foreman

Ros Bayley's Almost Traditional Tales – a variety of traditional tales available on CD with catchy raps integrated into the stories.

Flip-up Fairy Tales – a series of picture books with accompanying CDs featuring various traditional tales.

Fairytale Jumbles by Hilary Robinson – a series of stories made up from combinations of fairytales.

**Activity/Resource books**

A&C Black's Roald Dahl Series of Musicals – performance packs for schools featuring a range of traditional tales with a twist
A&C Black, (tel: 0207 758 0200)
– www.acblack.com

The Little Book of Nursery Rhymes, Sally Featherstone, 2002.
Featherstone Education (tel: 0207 758 0200)
– www.acblack.com/featherstone

The Little Book of Storytelling, Mary Medlicott, 2003.
Featherstone Education (tel: 0207 758 0200)
– www.acblack.com/featherstone

Maths in Stories, Judith Stevens, 2008.
BEAM Education (tel: 0207 684 3324)
– www.beam.co.uk

How to Enjoy Reading Aloud to Young Children, Edmund Pegge & Alison Shakespeare, 2007.
Southgate Publishers (tel: 01363 776889)
– www.southgatepublishers.co.uk

# Useful websites

National Literacy Trust
– www.literacytrust.org.uk and www.earlyreadingconnects.org.uk

Every Child Matters
– www.dcsf.gov.uk/everychildmatters

Department for Children Schools and Families
– www.nationalstrategies.standards.dcsf.gov.uk/earlyyears and www.standards.dfes.gov.uk/primary/teachingresources/literacy

The Basic Skills Agency
– www.basic-skills.co.uk

The Society for Storytelling
– www.sfs.org.uk

Seven Stories Centre for Children's Books
– www.sevenstories.org.uk

Booktrust
– www.booktrust.org.uk

Reading for Life
– www.readingforlife.org.uk

British Council
– www.britishcouncil.org/kids-stories-fairy-tales.htm - animated fairytales.

Nursery Rhymes and Silly Stuff
– www.smart-central.com - excellent range of nursery rhymes with words and tunes.

Children's Music.co.uk
– www.childrensmusic.co.uk/songs.html - downloadable children's songs.

# Resources

TTS Group
www.tts-group.co.uk
0800 318686
Storytelling resources: Fairytale glove and finger puppets; big books; E-books; story boxes; story prop sets; Bee-Bot fairytale cards; Bee-Bot fairytale mat; story sacks. Role play/small world: Fairytale mat and castle; fairy tale figures; character masks.

Cambridge Educational Toys
www.cambridgeeducationaltoys.com
01953 859520
Storytelling resources: Character masks; mitts for counting rhymes; character finger and hand puppets; puppet theatres; felt/magnetic storyboards; books.

Clever Clogs
www.cleverclogsgames.co.uk
01823 327836

Games: The Hare and the Tortoise sequencing game; Where's the Wolf letter recognition game; The Three Silly Goats Gruff story game; Three Little Pig Tales speaking and listening game.

Yellow Door
www.yellowdoor.net
0845 6035309
Come Alive Stories: Resource packs for traditional tales that include story cards, audio CDs and activity books for teachers, wooden character sets and interactive CD-ROMs. Story props and masks for a large number of traditional tales; small world resources; story boxes.

Amazon
www.amazon.co.uk
You will find all the books mentioned in this Little Book on Amazon.